# All About Water

by **Melvin Berger**

illustrated by **Paul Meisel**

**SCHOLASTIC INC.**

New York   Toronto   London   Auckland   Sydney

For Max, with love
—M.B.

With thanks to Dr. Anthony Ting, Stanford University,
for his assistance in preparing this book.

ISBN 0-590-46761-1

12 11 10 9 8 7 6 5 4 3 2 1     3 4 5 6 7 8/9

Printed in the U.S.A.          09

First Scholastic printing, October 1993

Water is everywhere.

You find it:

- in oceans, rivers, and lakes.
- in our homes and factories.
- in the ground and in the air we breathe.
- in our bodies and in the food we eat.

Water is one of the most common substances on Earth.
Yet water is also a very odd substance.

Sometimes water is a liquid.
The water you drink is liquid water.

Sometimes water is a solid.
The ice cube in your juice is solid water.

Sometimes water is a gas.
Clouds of hot steam are water
in the form of a gas.
All air contains water in the form of a gas.
This gas is called water vapor.

Water can be found in
three different forms.
Liquid, solid, and gas.

Liquid water has no fixed shape.
It flows from place to place.

You can change water from a liquid into a solid.
It's easy to do.

## DO IT YOURSELF

### Liquid Water into Solid Ice

Get a clean plastic margarine or cottage cheese tub.
Fill it halfway with liquid water.

Place the tub of water in a freezer.
Leave it there overnight.

Take out the tub.
What do you see?

The liquid water has become solid!

Water that is solid is called ice.
Liquid water becomes ice when it gets very cold.

Ice does not flow.
It is hard.
It has a definite shape.

Liquid water changes into water vapor, too.
The water vapor disappears into the air.
You can't see it or smell it, but it's there.

Would you like to change
liquid water into water vapor?

## DO IT YOURSELF

### Liquid Water into Water Vapor

Put a teaspoon of water in a saucer.
Put the saucer on a sunny windowsill.
Or set it on a shelf in a warm spot.
Leave the saucer until the next day.

Now look at the saucer.
What happened to the water?

It's all gone!
Where did it go?

The liquid water slowly changed into water vapor.
The water vapor went into the air.
And the liquid water disappeared from the saucer.

The change from liquid water into
water vapor is called *evaporation*.

Have you ever been caught in a rainstorm?
Lots of water comes pouring down.
The water flows along streets and roads.

The next day the water may be all gone.
Some of it flowed into sewers.
Some soaked into the ground.
But where did the rest of the water go?

The liquid rain water changed into water vapor.
It evaporated.
It became an invisible gas in the air.

Sometimes it takes a long time
for rain water to disappear.
But other times water disappears very quickly.
Here's how you can make water disappear
very quickly.

# DO IT YOURSELF

## From Liquid Water to Water Vapor

Put some water in a kettle.
Set the kettle on the stove.
Ask an adult to turn on high heat.

Wait a few minutes.
You'll see clouds coming from the kettle.
The clouds are water vapor.
Be careful.
The clouds are very hot.

Watch the water vapor mix with the air.

The water vapor disappears.
Soon the liquid water in the kettle will be all gone.
Ask an adult to turn off the heat before this
happens.

Now you know how to make water disappear.
Did you know you can also make water appear?

# DO IT YOURSELF

## From Water Vapor to Liquid Water

Take a clean, dry glass.
Fill it with ice cubes.
Place the glass on a table.

Wait about 10 minutes.
Now look at the outside of the glass.
Do you see tiny drops of water?
How did they get there?

The cold glass chilled the water vapor in the air.
The chilled water vapor changed into liquid water.
The liquid water formed the drops on the glass.

The change of water vapor into liquid water
is called *condensation*.

You made water appear from the air
by condensation.
Now you can also use water to make
things disappear.

## DO IT YOURSELF

### Making Salt Disappear

Fill a glass nearly full of water.
Add a teaspoon of salt to the water.
Stir the water.
The salt is gone.

Where did the salt go?
It disappeared in the water.
When something disappears in water
we say it *dissolves*.

Can you prove that the salt is in the water?
Dip your finger in the water.
Lick the tip of your finger.
How does it taste?
You can't see the salt.
But you sure can taste it!

The salt dissolved in the water.
Here's how to make the salt appear again.

## DO IT YOURSELF

### Making Salt Appear

Put a spoonful of the salt water in a saucer.
Place the saucer in a warm spot.
Leave it there for a day.
What happens?

The water disappears.
It evaporates into the air.

But it leaves tiny white specks on the saucer.
What are they?

Taste one of the little bits.
It's a grain of salt.

The water part of the salt water became
water vapor.
The water vapor escaped into the air.
Only the salt remained in the dish.

Water mostly flows down.
Rain, waterfalls, showers.
They all flow down.

Sometimes water flows up.
Water moves up in ocean waves and
water fountains.

But did you know that water
always flows up in plants?

## DO IT YOURSELF

### Watching Water Move Up

Get a stalk of celery, a glass of water,
and some red food coloring.
Add enough coloring to turn the water bright red.
Ask an adult to cut off the top and bottom
of the stalk.
Put the stalk into the water.

After an hour, take the celery out of the water.
Look closely.
Do you see thin red lines in the celery?

The colored water moves *up* through the celery.
It moves up through thin little tubes.

If you can't see the lines, hold the celery
in front of a bright light.
The light makes the red lines easier to see.

Water moves up through all plants.
Plants have roots in the ground.
The roots take in water.
From here the water moves up.
It goes to the:

- stems
- leaves
- flowers
- and fruits.

Plants contain lots of water.
So does your body.
Suppose you weigh 60 pounds.
More than 40 pounds of your weight is water!
You can watch some of the water
escape from inside your body.

# DO IT YOURSELF

## Water in Your Breath

Get a small mirror.
Hold it close to your lips.
Open your mouth as wide as you can.
Blow out.

Notice the foggy spot that forms on the mirror.
Rub your finger across that spot.
How does it feel?
Wet. The spot is liquid water.

Water vapor is in your body.
You blow out.
The water vapor in your breath
strikes the cold mirror.
The water vapor condenses and changes
into liquid water.
The liquid water forms the spot on the mirror.

The foods you eat contain water.
Even solid foods are full of water.
Tomatoes are 95 percent water.
Carrots are 90 percent water.
Potatoes are 80 percent water.
Bread is 30 percent water.

# DO IT YOURSELF

## Finding the Water in Food

Get slices of tomato, carrot, potato, and bread.
(You may also try other solid foods.)
Look at the size of each slice of food.
Touch it so you know how it feels.

Place the foods on a pan in the oven.
Ask an adult to turn on the oven to the
lowest heat.

Leave the food slices in the oven for about an hour.
The heat will change the water
in the food into water vapor.
The water vapor will come out of the food.

Ask the adult to take out the food slices
and turn the oven off.
Let the slices cool.

Look at each one.
See how much smaller they have become.

Touch each one.
Notice how different they feel without the water.

Some things — like wood — weigh less than water.
Other things — like steel — weigh more than water.

Things that weigh less than water
stay on top of water.
They float.

Things that weigh more than water
drop to the bottom of water.
They sink.

# DO IT YOURSELF

## Float or sink?

Collect a number of small items, such as:

- rock
- leaf
- pine cone
- acorn
- feather
- twig
- tennis ball
- bottle cap
- penny
- pencil

Fill a big bowl or pan with water.
Drop in the items one at a time.

Which ones float in the water?
Which ones sink?

Remember:
The floaters weigh *less* than the water they replace.
The sinkers weigh *more* than the water they replace.

Water is amazing.
It is liquid, solid, and gas.

It evaporates and disappears.

It condenses and appears.
It dissolves other things and makes them disappear.

It makes up most of our bodies.
It lets wood float and steel sink.

Every drop of water is made up of millions and millions of tiny bits.
These bits are called molecules.

The water molecules on Earth have been here for a very long time.
Ages ago, the dinosaurs drank millions of molecules of water.
Today, we drink millions of water molecules.
Some of the molecules we drink are the very same ones the dinosaurs drank long ago!